Renate Wagner-Wittula
Imperial Austrian Cuisine
Aus Kaisers Küche
The Best Recipes from the Austro-Hungarian Royal Kitchen
With Culinary Comments
by Christoph Wagner
Translated by Mark Hackworth & Paul Heinrichs

Buchvertrieb Joachim Klinger, Landwiedstr. 199, 4020 Linz,
Tel.Nr. ++43(0)732-382095

Production: Werbebüro G. Linecker
Graphics and Layout: Sieglinde Füreder
Cover-Design: Günter Linecker
Photos: Partnerstudios Christoph Goldmann, Friedrich Jansenberger,
Österreich Werbung
Props: Pia Steinwender
Studio Chefs: Alfred Schrot (Schrot & Korn), Konditorei Josef Kemetmüller
(Neuhofen/Krems)
Kitchenware: Firma Rechberger GesmbH, Linz
Printed by: Gorenjski Tisk

ISBN 3-7066-2187-8

Renate Wagner-Wittula

Imperial Austrian Cuisine
Aus Kaisers Küche

The Best Recipes from the Austro-Hungarian Royal Kitchen

With Culinary Comments
by Christoph Wagner

Translated by Mark Hackworth & Paul Heinrichs

EDITION LÖWENZAHN

Table of Contents

How Can You Still Cook Like a Kaiser Today?

In an era in which the vol-au-vent, or pies were stuffed to the brim, the capons roasted to crispy perfection, the exquisite sweets full of whipped cream, one rarely ever raised an objection when the shopping list was laden with dozens of eggs and masses of butter, or lard – at least not what nutrition was concerned. This type of royal cuisine, however, was irrelevant for the economically less fortune household.

Yet, much has changed since the royal days of heavenly cuisine. Although eggs are nowadays rarely regarded as a luxury because of the improved economical situation, today's health concerns are enough to scare off most knowledgeable consumers from unfavorable cholesterol bombs. The same holds true, by the way, for all kinds of animal fat, innards or overly fatty meat, not to mention the especially loved and nowadays rare fowl, such as the bunting and thrush, and obscure aquatic animals, such as the beaver or badger, which have disappeared altogether from menus due in large part to animal protection issues.

It was, therefore, the goal of this collection of recipes to provide the cookbook user with the ability to work imperial culinary magic without having to scuttle all nutritional awareness. Naturally, we couldn't omit a certain amount of so-called "opulent" ingredients, otherwise the taste would simply be unduly distorted.

Those who want imperial enjoyment while concurrently watching their figure are certainly allowed to use one or more reduced calorie products in place of the listed ingredients.

The same can be said for sizing-up portions – if not otherwise indicated, the recipe makes four average portions, which can of course be somewhat reduced in this age where thin is in. The recommended temperatures and cooking times are to be understood as general guidelines, especially with the desserts, where it's unimportant which flour is used and how large the eggs are or what type of oven is being used. Ideally, one should trust his own instincts what this concerns, which is invariably the most important and invaluable ingredient of every dish.

With that I wish you much success –
bon appétit!

Renate Wagner-Wittula

Completely Kaiser

The Habsburg lineage, who guided the fate of large parts of Europe between 1273–1918, although known to have been very conscientious, went down in history being regarded more as solemn bureaucrats. In fact, the Austrian dynasty can neither be seriously compared to the French Bourbons, nor to the famous Italian Royal House of Borgia to Medici. Nonetheless, one would not be doing the Habsburgs justice if one were to simply dismiss them as somber ascetics. On the contrary, most of them possessed a tremendous appetite. Some were fond of a simpler diet, while others proved to be food connoisseurs, if not gourmets. Thanks alone to his distinct stoutness, Kaiser Friederich III (1415–1493) was known not to refuse a good meal. Kaiser Ferdinand I (1503–1564) was not only a well-known sweet-tooth, but also enjoyed eating crab, escargot, as well as all types of fowl. In 1523 he even had a culinary school built on the Minoriten Square in Vienna for the children of the royal family. After he had retired into the San Jeronimo de Yuste cloister from the toils of his life wrought with prestige and power, Kaiser Karl V (1500–1588) corresponded with the outside world almost exclusively about topics like his own ample nourishment through pickled chicken, Flemish sausages, finely marbled veal and eel pie. Kaiser Karl VI (1685–1740), on the other hand, loved eating beaver tail with lemon sauce, grilled heron, as well as squirrel with cauliflower and strawberries.

In contrast, there were also admittedly Kaisers of the Habsburg lineage, who – in order to avoid criticism from their starving subjects – lionized a more meager diet. For example, the enlightened and sober Josef II (1741–1790) would invariably appear two hours late for meals to show everyone at the table his low opinion of pleasures of the flesh.

However, not even this brand of monarch could prevent the word "Kaiser" from becoming prominent in Viennese cuisine. This extends from "Kaiser" beer to the juicy, rind-laden "Kaiser" meat to the star-patterned "Kaiser" Roll and on to the legendary "Kaiser" Pancakes. "Kaiser" flour denotes the best wheat flour in the kitchen, "Kaiser" biscuits a soup complement made with lots of butter and cheese, "Kaiser" fish a char or young salmon, "Kaiser" pear an especially exquisite butter pear, "Kaiser" goulash a beef tenderloin goulash with buttered noodles, "Kaiser" schnitzel a veal cutlet flavored with parsley, sardines, capers and lemon juice, "Kaiser" café au lait a large mocha which is rounded off with honey and brandy instead of milk and egg yolks.

In short: in olden days Vienna, every petty official loved to govern his own "small Schönbrunn", be it even so small as a tiny burrow. More importantly, he also wanted to be a miniature Kaiser what the pleasures of the table were concerned. For this reason in particular, Viennese cuisine of old contains many "imperial" dishes modified by the middle-class. An abundant number of aristocrats such as the Esterhàzys, the Tegetthoffs, the Metternichs, the Auerspergs, or the Trautmansdorffs, just to name of few of the famous Austrian families, were allowed to link their names to these timeless dishes. Currently, these dishes may seem to be too heavy and overly lavish, which has more to do with today's changing lifestyles and habits than with their "imperial" character. Who nowadays is on the go with a horse the entire day, who pushes a plow for hours at a time, and what bureaucratic office, as they did during the reign of the Kaisers, could do without an elevator? Because one burned more calories in earlier times, one also had to consume more. One wasn't afraid to eat a torte prepared with sixteen eggs or pasta dough made with thirty-six eggs – at that time, the word cholesterol wasn't a familiar concept.

The following recipes are original recipes from the time of the Kaisers. They have been, however, carefully adapted – some more, some less – to today's dietary requirements. Therefore, they can also be thoroughly enjoyed as "imperial delights" in democratic times.

The Kaiser's Compulsive Nibbler

The name Barbara, pronounced in true Viennese dialect Waberl, went down in culinary history in the old city of the Kaisers. The most famous representative, namely a certain Barbara Roman, linked this name to fame during the reign of Empress Maria Theresia by taking it upon herself to discretely collect the abundant left-overs from the royal Viennese table and sell them cheaply in her inn "The Golden Ship" located on Spittel Mountain. What miracles she was able to work with the royal left-overs can be seen, by the way, in the legendary Eipeldauer letters, the contents of which reveal that the pheasants and capons actually flew from the royal kitchen to Spittel Mountain even after having been plucked and cooked.

Imperial Appetizers

Imperiale Vorspeisen

Fork Brunch for a Minnesinger

Even before the Imperial Court moved to Vienna, the City of the Danube was regarded as a European metropolis of high standing. The rich and art-loving Babenberg dukes attracted many artists from all over Europe. Among them was also the legendary minnesinger Tannhäuser who supposedly even had breakfast with Frau Venus. Mr. Tannhäuser was not only well-liked during the years 1235–1246 under the rule of Duke Friedrich II, he was even pampered by the officialdom. Furthermore, a noble piece of property was put at his disposal. Nonetheless, Tannhäuser suffered from an incurable shortage of money. In his songs, he sang sadly about how he had to gradually pawn his dwindling possessions. He simply indulged all too often in beautiful women, good wine, the bath houses, and above all in his beloved fork brunch. Therefore, it was not surprising to hear the Viennese innkeepers remark, as the minnesinger himself also candidly admitted, they would rather see him "going than coming".

Sophie's Pie

Sophienpastete
named after Archduchess Sophie of Austria (1805–1872),
mother of Kaiser Franz Joseph

Preparation:

The crêpes should be prepared first. Thoroughly mix all ingredients for the crêpe batter. Heat a mixture of butter and clarified butter in a flat pan, add a portion of the batter (just enough to cover the bottom of the pan) and brown – turn crêpe and fry until other side is also golden brown. Finish making the rest of the crêpes one by one. Now combine the eggs and cream, whisk thoroughly and season with salt and nutmeg. Cut the ham into thin strips. Grease a suitable baking pan or casserole dish with melted butter and cover the bottom of the pan with a layer of crêpes, making sure that the crêpes extend over the edges. Spread a few of the strips of ham over the crêpes and top with whisked cream, followed by another layer of crêpes. Repeat this procedure until all ingredients have been used up. Fold the edges of the crêpes which extend beyond the rim of the pan over the top in shingle-like fashion and top with a few slivers of butter. Bake in an oven preheated between 350–400 °F (180–200 °C) for approximately 45 minutes. Sprinkle grated cheese over the pie about 10 minutes before the baking time has elapsed and bake until golden brown.

Ingredients:

3 eggs
250 ml (8 fluid oz) cream
400 g (14 oz) sliced ham
salt
nutmeg
butter to grease pan
grated cheese for topping
for the crêpes:
150 g (5 oz) flour
300 ml (9 fluid oz) milk
5 eggs
salt
butter and clarified butter

Archduke Johann Pie

Erzherzog-Johann-Pastete
named after Archduke Johann von Habsburg-Lothringen (1782–1859), regent of the German Empire

Ingredients:

makes approx. 4 large or 8 small pies

For the dough:

- 1 egg
- 1 egg yolk
- 300 g (9 oz) flour
- 150 g (5 oz) butter
- dash of vinegar
- 4 Tbs. cream
- small pie pans
- butter for greasing

for the filling:

- 250 g (9 oz) sautéed or baked veal
- 5–6 Tbs. fresh peas (or frozen if fresh not available)
- 1 Tbs. butter
- 1 Tbs. flour
- beef broth or water
- one egg yolk to thicken
- nutmeg
- salt
- freshly ground pepper
- sprig of parsley for garish

Preparation:

Combine flour, egg, egg yolks, butter, cream and a dash of vinegar and quickly knead into a smooth dough. Let sit approximately one half hour. Then roll the dough to the thickness of a knife handle and divide the dough so that one piece fits in each pie pan. Grease each pie pan with butter and line with dough. Preheat the oven to 400 °F (200 °C) and lightly bake the pies 20–25 minutes. In the meantime, make the filling by blanching the peas in salted water and finely chopping or mincing the veal. Melt butter in a saucepan, then stir in flour and minced meat - braise briefly with beef broth or water. Let mixture reduce before adding nutmeg, salt and freshly ground pepper to taste. Stir in peas and remove pan from heat. Thicken sauce with egg yolks. The pies which have finished baking in the meantime and have cooled slightly are now filled with the stuffing and browned for several minutes in an oven preheated between 400–425 °F (200–225 °C). Garnish the finished pies with a sprig of parsley and serve in pan.

Eggs à la Metternich

Eier à la Metternich
named after the Chancellor of the House Metternich, Royal Chancellor of Austria and Head of State Prince Clemens Wenzel Lothar von Metternich (1773–1859)

Preparation:

For the meat patties, begin by mincing the bacon and veal , add one egg, bread crumbs, and spices – mix well. Form four flat patties from the mixture, fry on both sides in hot fat in a flat pan and after which reduce heat to low. Add one dash of vinegar and a pinch of salt to approximately 1 1/2 liters water (48 fluid oz) and bring to a boil. Crack the eggs and let them carefully slide one by one into the boiling water. Use a spoon to pull the egg whites over the egg yolks so that the yolks are completely enveloped by the egg whites. Gently remove the poached eggs, immerse them briefly in cold water, drain excess water, trim all unsightly egg white strands and keep warm over low heat. For the sauce, place egg yokes in a double-boiler (let 1 pot of water simmer, place smaller pot inside first pot – ingredients are then added to smaller pot), add oil drop by drop and stir until the egg yokes slowly begin to stiffen. Add mustard, salt and sugar and continue stirring until the sauce thickens. Dress each patty with a poached egg and nap (drizzle) with sauce. Garnish with chopped parsley.

Ingredients:

50 g (2 oz) bacon
250 g (9 oz) veal
1 egg
1 Tbs. bread crumbs
marjoram
pepper
cardamom
clarified butter or oil for frying

for the poached eggs:

4 eggs
vinegar
salt

for the sauce:

2–3 egg yolks
2 Tbs. oil
mustard
salt
sugar
chopped parsley for garnish

Tegetthoff-Omelettes

Tegetthoff-Omelette
named after the Austrian Admiral Wilhelm Freiherr von Tegetthoff (1827–1871)

Preparation:

First, thoroughly mix the eggs with the melted butter and season with a pinch of salt. Melt some butter in a crêpe-pan and pour in just enough of the mixture for one omelette. Fry the first side of the omelette while continuously tilting the pan from side to side. Remove the pan from the heat as soon as the visible side of the omelette begins to set, fold both sides evenly towards the center and quickly set aside (keep warm) – repeat this procedure while cooking another three omelettes. Finely dice the cooked green beans, the cauliflower, as well as the chicken, slice the mushrooms and sauté lightly in butter. Allow butter to become foamy, stir in flour and add chicken broth. Let the light roux thicken – remove from heat. Stir in vegetables along with the peas and chicken and season with salt and pepper. Lastly, thicken with egg yolks and whipping cream. Fill the omelettes with the roux-mixture and roll or fold shut.

Ingredients:

for the omelettes:

- 8 eggs
- 1 Tbs. melted butter
- salt
- butter

for the filling:

- 100 g (3 1/2 oz) cooked fresh peas (or frozen, if fresh not available)
- 100 g (3 1/2 oz) cooked green beans
- 100 g (3 1/2 oz) cooked cauliflower
- 250 g (9 oz) cooked chicken
- 50 g (2 oz) fresh mushrooms
- 2 Tbs. each of butter and flour for the roux
- chicken broth
- butter for frying
- 1 egg yolk
- 100 ml (3 fluid oz) whipping cream
- salt
- pepper

Kaiser Sausages in a Blanket

Kaiserwürstchen im Schlafrock

Preparation:

Mince the boneless chicken meat, finely chop the smoked tongue, soak the roll in milk, squeeze out the milk and chop finely. Clean and coarsely chop the mushrooms and goose liver and lightly sauté each separately in a small amount of butter. Thoroughly mix the chicken and veal with the coarsely chopped roll, the chopped tongue, egg yolk(s), diced mushrooms, goose liver and the chopped pistachios and season with salt and pepper. Form small sausages from this mixture on a floured surface, fry on all sides in hot oil and set aside to cool. In the meantime, roll out and divide the puff pastry in such a way that one sausage can be rolled up in each piece. Lay the rolled sausages on a sheet tray lined with wax paper – lightly brush the puff pastry with egg. Preheat the oven to 400 °F (200 °C) and bake 15–20 minutes until golden brown. The sausages can be eaten as a snack or sliced and used as a decorative for a more opulent breakfast dish.

Ingredients:

makes 15–20 sausages

- 200 g (7 oz) minced veal
- 300 g (10 oz) boneless chicken breast and thigh meat
- 100 g (3 1/2 oz) smoked cow tongue (cooked)
- 50 g (2 oz) mushrooms
- 100 g (3 1/2 oz) goose liver (or chicken liver if not available)
- 1 roll
- 1–2 egg yolks
- 80 g (3 oz) chopped pistachios
- milk or water for soaking
- butter or oil for frying
- puff pastry
- flour for dusting
- 1 egg for glaze
- salt
- pepper

Castle Gödöllö-Doughnuts

Schloß Gödöllö-Pogatscherl
named after the summer residence of Kaiser Franz Joseph and Empress Elisabeth in Budapest-Hatvan, where the royal couple from Hungary resided many a summer from 1868 on

Preparation:

Dissolve yeast in warm milk, add a small amount of flour and let rise for a short time. In the meantime, finely chop or mince the greaves, spread them over a counter-top and sprinkle with flour. Add egg, cream, wine and seasonings to greaves – combine with the milk, yeast and flour mixture and work into a dough. Roll the dough thin, ball together, and roll out thin once more. Repeat this procedure three times before balling the dough together one last time – allow to rise in a warm place for exactly one hour. Roll the dough out once again. Be sure not to roll the dough out too thin, approximately 2–3 cm (3/4" - 1 1/4"). Cut out doughnuts with a round cookie-cutter and place on a sheet tray lined with baking paper. With a sharp knife, make a grill-like design (#) on the tops of the doughnuts and brush lightly with egg. Let the doughnuts rise once more and then bake in an oven pre-heated to 350 °F (180 °C) for 30–40 minutes until golden brown. Greave-doughnuts can be enjoyed as a delicious snack, a warm appetizer or even as a tasty side-dish.

Ingredients:

20 g yeast
a bit of milk for dissolving
350 g (12 oz) greaves
400 g (14 oz) flour
1 egg
2 Tbs. cream
1 Tbs. wine
salt
pepper
1 egg for coating

THE KAISER'S HUNTING VITTLES

Kaisers Jagdproviant

Ingredients:

- 1 loaf French bread (best with smooth surface)
- 150 g (5 oz) butter
- 150 g (5 oz) drained Gervais cheese or curd cheese (quark)
- salt
- pepper
- mustard
- anchovy paste
- 300–400 g (11–14 oz) ham
- smoked pork and/or smoked cow tongue
- 400 g (14 oz) Edam cheese
- 3–4 hard-boiled eggs
- 100 g (3 1/2 oz) chopped pickles
- chopped chives to taste

Preparation:

Cut one end off French bread with a long knife and hollow out the loaf with a spoon to the width of a finger. The bread removed with the spoon should now be cut finely and set aside. Finely cube the ham, smoked pork, cow tongue, cheese and pickles. Separate the egg whites from the yolks of the hard boiled eggs and likewise cube, after which pass the yolks through a sieve. In a pot, melt butter and stir until foamy, mix in quark or Gervais as well as the sieved egg yolks and the finely cut bread – flavor with salt, pepper, mustard and anchovy paste. At this point, mix all of the ingredients for the filling together and carefully insert the filling into the hollowed-out loaf and compact firmly. Reattach the severed end and wrap in a moist towel or in aluminum foil and refrigerate overnight. Cut the French loaf in 1" (about the width of a thumb) slices and serve.

"Häferlgucker" on Patrol

The Habsburgs, despite the many "imperial" dishes named after them, were seldom what one would call "sensuous". Kaiser Leopold, who was cast from a similar mold, passed several "anti-luxury laws" against excessively opulent banquets at weddings, baptisms, and funerals and also kept a short leash on his subjects what pleasures of the flesh were concerned. Since people of that day refused to take the Kaiser's laws and decrees all too literally, the Kaiser actually recruited a special task force. These "gourmet-agents" consisted of specially appointed kitchen inspectors who enforced compliance with the "luxury laws" even in the households of low ranking officials. The tongue of the commoner coined a nickname for these kitchen-kibitzers: Häferlgucker, literally "cup peepers". Kaiser Leopold himself seemed to also not have followed his own laws to the letter. He was personally a patron of gallant festivities and thought nothing of showing-up with his wife disguised as innkeepers at the Königsegg'schen Palace in Gumpendorf on the 26th of June, 1698 on the occasion of a masquerade ball honoring Czar Peter the Great. The ball had an "Imperial tavern" theme.

Imperial Soup Delights

Kaiserlich-königliche Suppengenüsse

Kaiser Consommé

Kaiser-Consommé

Preparation:

To begin, cube or mince the beef and add to 2 liters of cold water. Then stir in the beef bones, root vegetables and the 1/2 onion, bring to a boil and let simmer at least 1 1/2 hours (should not exceed 2 hours). Let the soup cool and skim off the layer of fat. Add egg whites to 250 ml cold water and stir well, incorporate into soup while stirring constantly. Bring to a boil once again, and let simmer until the soup is clear. Strain through a cheese cloth or kitchen towel – season if necessary.
In the meantime, prepare the body of the soup by mincing the veal together with a roll that has been lightly soaked in milk – combine with egg, egg yolks, spices, and a shot of heavy cream and mix well. Grease a small pan with butter, sprinkle with bread crumbs and spread in the mixture to the thickness of 1" (about the width of a thumb). Preheat the oven between 350–400 °F (180–200 °C) and lightly bake approximately 15 minutes. Remove immediately from pan as soon as the mixture has slightly cooled and cut out in any desired shape, diamonds or stars for example, and incorporate into soup. Garnish with chopped parsley.

Ingredients:

makes 6 portions

500 g (1 lb.) beef (remove all connective tissue)

beef bones

root vegetables (parsley, carrots, celery stalk)

1/2 onion

2 l (64 fluid oz) water

3 egg whites

250 ml (8 fluid oz) cold water

salt

for the soup body:

200 g (7 oz) sautéed veal

1 roll

milk

1 egg

2 egg yolks

salt

pepper

nutmeg

shot of heavy cream

butter

bread crumbs

chopped parsley for garnish

His Highness's Steamed Soufflé Strip Soup

Durchlauchts Dunstkochsuppe

Preparation:

Melt the butter in a pot until foamy, mix in the potatoes and the diced smoked pork and season with salt and nutmeg. Separate the egg yolks from the whites and stir them into the potato mixture. Beat the whites until stiff. Gently fold in flour and whisked egg whites and season if necessary. Brush a small pie or soufflé pan with butter and sprinkle with flour – add mixture. Place in double-boiler and simmer at medium heat for 45–60 minutes (place in oven if necessary). Turn the soufflés upside down to remove and let cool. Carefully cut into thin strips and sprinkle with parsley. Heat up the broth and serve along with the Kaiser-Soufflé strips.

Ingredients:

makes 6 portions

1 l (32 fluid oz) concentrated beef broth

2 Tbs. butter

100 g (3 1/2 oz) potatoes (boiled and passed through a sieve)

50 g (2 oz) finely chopped ham or smoked pork (cooked)

2 eggs

1 tsp. flour

nutmeg

salt

butter

flour for dusting

chopped parsley

SOUP FOR THE IMPERIAL BALL

Hofburgballsuppe

Preparation:

Coarsely chop the bacon, slice the root vegetables and the onion, then disjoint the drawn stewing chicken. Afterwords, throw all the ingredients into a pot and sauté until the root vegetables and bacon begin to brown. Now fill with enough cold water to cover ingredients and simmer over medium heat for 7–8 hours. After this time has elapsed, carefully strain the soup through a fine-mesh-sieve or an Etamin (a fine cloth, or cheese cloth) so that it's clear and not cloudy. In earlier times the soup was served "straight" in small bowls, but nowadays it can also be served with a fitting complement of course, such as the Austrian Kaiserschöberln, a special type of biscuit often used to complement a soup.

Ingredients:

makes 6 portions

- 250 g (9 oz) bacon
- 250 g (9 oz) beef and calves' liver
- 1 stewing chicken
- beef bones
- 1 cow spleen
- 1 onion
- root vegetables (celery stalk, carrots, parsley, etc.)
- salt
- pepper

Anna-Plochl-Soup

Anna-Plochl-Suppe
named after the morganatic wife of Archduke Johann,
a postmaster's daughter whom he met in Ausseerland

Ingredients:

- 1 l (32 fluid oz) beef broth
- 300-400 g (10–14 oz) of root vegetables (celery stalk, carrots, parsley, etc.)
- kohlrabi
- cauliflower
- Brussels sprouts
- green beans
- mushrooms or peas
- 3 Tbs. coarsely chopped bacon
- 2 Tbs. butter
- oil
- pinch of sugar
- salt
- pepper
- 4 large or 8 small slices of white bread
- a sharp or tangy cheese

Preparation:

Either dice or cut vegetables and root vegetables into thin strips according to taste. Boil the root vegetables and all of the other vegetables except for the mushrooms and peas (these will be cooked separately for just a few minutes) briefly in salted water – vegetables should remain crispy. Drain vegetables. Melt butter in a pot, stir in sugar and let slightly brown. Add a small amount of beef broth along with the vegetables and sauté 5–10 minutes. Now stir in the cooked mushrooms and peas and allow to once again cook briefly. Add remaining beef broth. Let thoroughly cook and finally season with salt and pepper. In the meantime, fry the chopped bacon in hot oil until crisp. Top the slices of white bread with the cheese and let lightly brown in oven. Ladle soup into small bowl, sprinkle the crisped bacon over the cheese croutons and carefully lay them in the soup. Serve immediately.

Kaiser-Biscuit-Soup

Kaiserschöberlsuppe

Preparation:

Separate the egg whites from the yolks. Melt butter in a pot and stir in milk, flour and egg yolks to form a dough. Add salt, nutmeg and grated cheese. Whip the egg whites until stiff and likewise mix in. Spread the mixture in a suitable pan lined with wax-paper (or a pan greased with butter and dusted with flour) to the thickness of 1" – about the width of a finger – and bake in an oven preheated between 400–425 °F (200–220 °C) for about 15 minutes until golden brown. Let cool and then cut into rhombuses or squares as desired. Either warm the Kaiser biscuits and serve separately on a tray along with the soup, or add them directly to the soup and warm for a few seconds – serve immediately.

Ingredients:

makes 6 portions

- 1 1/2 l (48 fluid oz) beef broth
- 3 Tbs. butter at room temperature
- 2 Tbs. milk
- 3 eggs
- 4 Tbs. flour
- nutmeg
- salt
- 2 Tbs. grated cheese
- butter for greasing
- flour for dusting

Chicken Soup à la Habsburg

Hühnersuppe à la Habsburg

Preparation:

For the roux, melt butter in a pot, add flour, stir in chicken broth and let cook at least half an hour. Clean and slice mushrooms and sauté lightly in a small amount of butter. Pass the cooked peas through a sieve. Add the sautéed mushrooms to the roux mixture and continue to cook over low heat. In the meantime, combine the sieved peas, egg yolk, and whipping cream, then stir these ingredients into the roux mixture along with the finely chopped chicken – remove from heat. Season with salt and freshly ground pepper according to taste. If desired, the chicken soup can also be served with croutons.

Ingredients:

makes 4–6 portions

1–1 1/2 l (32–48 fluid oz) chicken broth

1–2 Tbs. butter and 2 Tbs. flour

300 g (10 oz) cooked, finely chopped chicken (cooked and chopped giblets can also be used if desired)

100 g (3 1/2 oz) fresh mushrooms

150 g (5 oz) cooked fresh peas (if fresh not available, use frozen)

1 egg yolk

100 ml (3 fluid oz) whipping cream

salt

pepper

butter

The Kaiser's Fast Food

Kaiser Franz Joseph, having been conservative in manner and taste, would certainly not have appreciated fast food in today's sense of the word. Aside from this, though, his food just couldn't be served fast enough. The Kaiser gave his guests and cooks just an hour's time for a twelve course meal at the royal table, which was set for up to 25 people. He would then suddenly stand up and march into the neighboring lounge along with his startled guests to indulge in cigar smoking, which he obviously enjoyed more than the meal.

THE KAISER'S FAVORITE SOUP

Kaisers Lieblingssuppe

Preparation:

For the roux, melt 1–2 Tbs. butter in a pot until it becomes foamy, add flour and let lightly brown. Slowly stir in beef or veal stock and thoroughly cook. Sweat the onions in butter, add the chopped vegetables and steam briefly (vegetables should remain crisp). Mix in the diced veal tongue, thymus and chicken meat. Season with grated nutmeg, salt and freshly ground pepper and add roux. Bring once again to a boil and remove from heat. Immediately stir in heavy cream and egg yolk. Garnish with finely chopped parsley and serve.

Ingredients:

makes 4–6 portions

- 1–1 1/2 l (32-48 fluid oz) beef or veal stock
- 1–2 Tbs. butter
- 2 Tbs. flour
- 150 g (5 oz) cooked veal tongue
- 150 g (5 oz) skinned and blanched calves' thymus
- 150 g (5 oz) boiled or fried skinless chicken breast
- 1/2 onion
- root vegetables (carrot, celery stalk, parsley)
- artichoke hearts according to taste
- peas
- cauliflower
- button or Chinese mushrooms
- nutmeg
- salt
- freshly ground pepper
- butter
- 150 ml (4 fluid oz) heavy cream
- 1 egg yolk
- parsley

Breadcrumb Soup

Panadelsuppe
there was already mention made of this classic Austrian bread soup in the tried and true Viennese cookbook "Wienerischen bewährten Koch-Buch" in 1772

Preparation:

Remove crust from rolls or white bread and cube bread. Soak the cubed bread in a small amount of beef broth and whisk – ideally, the bread-mass should be passed through a sieve. Sauté the bread-mass in a small amount of butter and let lightly brown. Now add the beef broth. Season with salt and pepper, bring to a boil and whisk thoroughly. After you have removed the pot from the stove, thicken the soup by stirring in the whisked egg yolks. Serve the soup in cups or bowls and garnish with chopped chives.

Ingredients:

- 3–4 day old rolls or the corresponding amount of white bread
- 1 l (32 fluid oz) beef broth
- 2–3 egg yolks
- butter
- salt
- pepper
- chopped chives for garnish

The Princess Who Wrote a Cookbook

The fact that his wife was rolling in money, but in the end was still of middle class origin, caused the Habsburg Archduke Ferdinand II of Tyrol all sorts of family discord. For years he had to keep his marriage to Philippine Welser (1527–1580), who was as beautiful as she was intelligent, from the public. This went on until there was nothing left for him to do but officially acknowledge their marriage. It has since become known that the Archduke's choice was certainly not a bad one. Frau Philippine was not only as faithful a wife as she was circumspect, but also wrote a pharmacopoeia and cookbook that circulated well beyond the walls of the royal court of Innsbruck and can be found today in the national library. Just like her husband, whose orgies of eating and drinking were infamous, Philippine was also never one to refuse a good meal, though she seemed to never have had problems with her figure. A contemporary reflects with flattering words on her exceptionally fine physique, "She had such a soft throat that you could almost see the red Burgundy wine flow down when she drank."

Terlan Wine Soup

Terlaner Weinsuppe

Preparation:

Thoroughly heat the beef broth and wine in a sauce pan, stir in the whipping cream, the egg yolks and the spices. Reduce heat to low, otherwise the whipping cream may curdle, and whisk until the soup has a creamy consistency. In the meantime, toast the cubed roll in hot butter in a pan. Ladle the prepared wine soup into cups or bowls, top with the crispy croûtons and sprinkle generously with cinnamon – serve immediately.

Ingredients:

- 1/2 l (16 fluid oz) concentrated beef broth
- 250 ml (8 fluid oz) Terlan wine (or any dry white wine)
- 250 ml (8 fluid oz) whipping cream
- 5 egg yolks
- salt
- cinnamon
- cubed day old roll for garnish

O Olio mio

Olio or Oglio stew can be traced back to the Iberian Ollapotrida. It then made its way from the Spanish branch of the Habsburg lineage to Vienna, where it was prepared in four large kettles. The stew was soon regarded worldwide as a unique specialty of the royal Viennese kitchen and was served primarily at the royal balls in Vienna. Olio stew was as popular with diplomats as it was with personnel and was made to serve up to 2000 people. It was made out of beef, veal, innards, wild game, ducks, geese, partridges, doves, chicken, plenty of root vegetables, and Spanish chestnuts. Because it was thought to be improper to eat meat in "soup" in earlier days, the higher ranking officials were served straight liquid in cups while the meat of the stew was distributed among the greedily waiting servants and cook's helpers.

Entrées under the Sign of the Double-Eagle

Hauptgerichte im Zeichen des Doppeladlers

Castle Tyrol Trout

Forelle Schloß Tyrol
named after the seat of the Habsburgs in South Tyrol

Ingredients:

4 cleaned trout
milk
flour
salt
vegetable oil
lemon peel for garnish
for the sauce:
2 egg yolks
approx. 250 ml (8 fluid oz) oil
mustard
lemon juice
salt
pepper
sugar
Worcestershire sauce
tomato paste
ground horseradish

Preparation:

The cleaned trout should be well salted on both sides. Dip trout in milk and flour on both sides. In an appropriately sized pan, heat up a sufficient amount of oil to completely immerse the trout and fry until golden-brown on both sides. Remove trout from oil and pat dry with a paper towel. Garnish with lemon peel and serve with the already prepared mayonnaise sauce.

For the sauce, first combine the egg yolks with a small amount of mustard, a shot of lemon juice, salt, pepper and stir until smooth. Now slowly add the oil drop by drop while stirring constantly until the mayonnaise binds. Flavor with a pinch of sugar, a bit of Worcestershire sauce, tomato paste and freshly grated horseradish.

Recommended Side Dishes: buttered potatoes, lamb's lettuce salad with bacon bits

RADZIWILL WALLEYE

Schill Radziwill

named after an old Lithuanian line of nobility that was raised to royal rank in 1547

Ingredients:

1 walleye (pike-perch) of about 1 1/2 kg (3 lb.)
root vegetables (parsley, celery stalk, carrots etc.)
peppercorns
salt
beef broth or water
1–2 Tbs. cold butter
for the stuffing: approx. 250 g (9 oz) pike filet
1 Tbs. butter
1 Tbs. flour
approx. 125 ml (4 fluid oz) milk
1 egg yolk
salt

Preparation:

The walleye should first be gutted, scaled and removed of all fins and deboned in order to be stuffed. It is recommended that you ask your fish vendor to professionally prepare the filet for this purpose. For the stuffing, the pike filet should be first carefully deboned and then finely minced. Melt butter in a saucepan, add flour and milk, and stir into a smooth Béchamel sauce – let cool. Stir in the egg yolk, minced pike filet and season. Preheat the oven between 350–400 °F (180–200 °C). Fill the walleye with the pike stuffing and sew shut. Salt the outside of the fish well and place in a saucepan on top of the coarsely chopped root vegetables and peppercorns. Bake in oven at high heat. While the fish cooks for around 1 hour, frequently baste with water or beef broth. Remove the baked fish, drain the liquid and set aside. If necessary, baste once more with broth or water and reduce. Thicken the sauce by quickly stirring in pieces of cold butter after removing the saucepan from the heat.

Recommended Side Dish: parsley potatoes and a fresh salad

Kaiser Ferdinand in the Land of Milk and Honey

When Kaiser Ferdinand moved to Vienna from the Netherlands with his entire entourage, some of his retinue couldn't believe their eyes at having landed in such a paradise. "There is such an over-abundance of resources that there's almost not enough room for them all and it can be embarrassing at times," wrote the Spanish nobleman Christobal de Castillejo, a trusted friend of the Kaiser. He went into raptures about obtaining "crabs in abundance, the most beautiful that I've ever seen." Fish, fowl, wild game and artichokes supposedly came from Enzesfeld on the Triesting near Leobersdorf; from Rodaun on the other hand, he regularly obtained kids (young goats), chickens, buttered baked goods and little pies with towers and castles along with other such baked goods, small sugared pretzels, meat pies and quince cheese.

Hradschin Carp

Hradschin Karpfen
named after the castle in Prague where many of the Habsburgs resided

Preparation:

Add vinegar, peppercorns, bay leaf and coarsely chopped onion to a pot of salted water and let rapidly boil for 5 minutes – reduce heat. Add the carp filets and let cook just under the boiling point for 8–10 minutes depending on water temperature. Remove the filets from water, cover with aluminum foil and set aside. Keep stock for later use. In the meantime, heat the clarified butter for the sauce in an appropriate pan and lightly brown the gingerbread crumbs at low heat. Add the almonds, nuts, prunes, raisins (chopped if desired), and finally stir in the honey. Before the sauce begins to stick, add the fish stock one spoonful at a time until the sauce has reached a creamy, almost thick consistency. Pour in the dark beer and bring once again to boil until the sauce has considerably thickened. At the most, a small amount of prune purée may be added according to taste, which will give the sauce an added lightly sweet-piquant character. Finally, lay the carp filets in the sauce, flip once and warm-up briefly at low heat.
Recommended Side Dish: Bohemian dumplings

Ingredients:

4 200 g (7 oz) carp filets
approx. 750 ml (24 fluid oz) water
125 ml (4 fluid oz) vinegar
peppercorns
1 bay leaf
1 small onion
salt
for the sauce:
2 Tbs. clarified butter
2 Tbs. honey
80 g (3 oz) gingerbread crumbs
60 g (2 oz) slivered almonds
1 Tbs. chopped prunes
1 Tbs. chopped nuts
2 tsp. raisins
approx. 125 ml (4 fluid oz) dark beer
plum purée (optional)

Christofle
FRANCE

KAISERSCHNITZEL

Kaiserschnitzel

Preparation:

Carefully pound out the veal cutlets, make small incisions on the edges, salt on both sides and flour one of the sides. Heat up the clarified butter or oil and beginning with the floured side, fry both sides for a total of 6–8 minutes at high heat until golden brown. Remove the fried schnitzel from the pan and set aside. Add approximately 1 tsp. flour to the remaining drippings, ladle in beef broth or veal drippings and heavy cream and bring to a boil. After a few minutes, strain the sauce and refine with capers, parsley, lemon juice and peel. Finally, stir the cream into the sauce and lay the schnitzel in the now completed "Kaiser Sauce" and warm-up on both sides.
Recommended Side Dish: buttered rice with ham and peas

Ingredients:

- 4 veal cutlets
- 100 ml (3 fluid oz) of beef broth or veal drippings
- 100 ml (3 fluid oz) heavy cream
- 1 tsp. chopped capers
- juice from 1/2 lemon
- grated lemon peel
- chopped parsley
- 2 Tbs. cream
- salt
- flour
- clarified butter or oil

Roast Nut of Veal – Monarch Style

Kalbsnüßchen auf Regenten-Art

Preparation:

Cut a wide pocket in the nut of veal for the stuffing, or have this professionally prepared by your butcher. For the stuffing, soak the roll in milk or water, press out liquid. Now mince the roll or pass it through a sieve. Melt the butter in a pan, sauté the onions and add the chopped mushrooms, and sauté as well - then let cool. Mix all ingredients for the stuffing thoroughly and season, and if necessary mince once again. Rub salt and pepper onto all sides of the roast, carefully stuff and sew shut. In the meantime, preheat the oven to 400 °F (200 °C). Brown the roast on all sides along with the root vegetables in a saucepan, then bake in an oven for approximately ninety minutes. Baste often with beef broth or water. While baking, the heat should be gradually reduced to 340 °F (170 °C). Remove the prepared roast and keep warm. Bring the remaining juices – minus the root vegetables – to a boil in a sauce pan and bind with 1 Tbs. flour, or cold butter if necessary. If desired, the root vegetables can also be sautéed briefly in a light roux, augmented with broth and finally strained. Now top the roast with the already prepared sauce.

Recommended Side Dish: new potatoes or salad potatoes with tomato salad.

Ingredients:

1 nut of veal (pope's eye) weighing approx. 1 kg (2 lb.)

1 batch root vegetables

salt

pepper

beef broth

butter or oil

flour and/or butter for finishing sauce

for the stuffing:

200 g (7 oz) finely minced veal

1 roll

1–2 egg yolks

1/2 finely chopped onion

150 g (5 oz) chopped mushrooms

1 Tbs. chopped parsley

1 chopped garlic clove

salt

pepper

milk or water

butter

Leg for a Kaiser

Kaiserschlegel

Preparation:

Spread the finely chopped veal bones evenly in a pan, cut the smoked bacon into thin strips and wrap around and fasten to the skinned nut of veal with the help of a larding needle or a long sharp knife. Season the larded roast with salt and freshly ground pepper, and if necessary use kitchen string to sew it shut. Finally lay the roast in the pan with the chopped bones with the "best" side facing down. If butter is used to baste the meat, it should be melted separately; if oil is used, do not first heat, but rather pour it directly over the roast. Now sear the roast over intense heat, reduce heat and then continue cooking. In the meantime, however, you have to be watchful that there is always liquid in the pan. As soon as the liquid has evaporated, add water or soup immediately! After about 50–60 minutes turn the roast, let finish cooking for approximately 1 hour depending on size of roast. Baste frequently. Remove the roast from pan, set aside and keep warm. Now finish the sauce. To do this, sprinkle flour over the bones, mix the cream with the beef broth or water and pour in with bones. Let the sauce thoroughly cook, remove bones, strain and put the finishing touches on by adding the sardine filets, capers, lemon juice and parsley.

Recommended Side Dish: rice and vegetables according to season – such as peas, cauliflower or asparagus

Ingredients:

makes 4–6 portions

1-1 1/2 kg (2–3 lb.) leg of veal, veal fricandeau, or nut of veal (pope's eye)

approx. 500 g (1 1b) chopped veal bones

4–5 Tbs. oil or butter

150 g (5 oz) whole smoked bacon

1 Tbs. flour

salt

freshly ground pepper

200 ml (6 1/2 fluid oz) cream

beef broth or water

1 tsp. chopped capers

1 tsp. chopped sardine filets

lemon juice

chopped parsley

The Kaiser's Mirror

Kaiser Franz Joseph was anything but hard to please. That is, if we can believe the royal gardener at his majesty's castle in Schönbrunn, Maria Thuma, who was occasionally allowed to cook for the Kaiser. She maintained that he "was content with just a few small pieces of beef." With boiled rump roast – known to everyone to be the Kaiser's favorite meal – however, it was a different story. It had to be so tender that it could be cut with a spoon. On such an occasion, Franz Joseph was in the habit of laying his elegantly polished knife aside and for the remainder of the meal using it merely as a mirror for plucking his mustache.

Boiled Rump Roast

Tafelspitz

Preparation:

Rinse the beef and the beef bones with tepid water before using. Bring an adequate amount of water to a boil, and add the roast and the beef bones. Now rinse the root vegetables, cut the onions in half and fry in a pan without adding oil until dark brown. After the roast has cooked for about 40-50 minutes add the fried onions, root vegetables, remaining vegetables and seasonings to the beef – continue cooking 1–1 1/2 hours over medium-low heat until the meat is tender. Remove the roast from the pot, cut meat into slices against the grain and keep warm. The vegetables can also be cut into strips and served along with the broth if desired. If the broth is served, it should first be seasoned to taste and finally strained through a cheese cloth. According to an old Viennese tradition, the rump roast was garnished with slices of beef marrow which were briefly cooked separately in broth. They were then, as was the case in Ewald Plachutta's famous Hietzinger Brewery, served on toasted dark bread. However you choose to serve the rump roast, it should be sprinkled with chopped chives and coarse salt.

Recommended Side Dishes: fried potatoes, green beans with dill sauce or cream of spinach and a warm chive sauce or bread horseradish sauce

Ingredients:

makes approx. 4–5 servings

1 kg (2 lb.) boneless rump roast (or boneless rib roast, pot roast, boneless sirloin etc.)

beef bones

salt

1 large batch of root vegetables (carrots, parsley, celery stalk etc.)

1 onion

1 small leek

2 small tomatoes (optional)

2 pressed garlic cloves

1 bay leaf

peppercorns

4–5 slices beef marrow and 4–5 slices dark bread

chopped chives

coarse salt

Prince Rohan Beef Tenderloin

Lungenbraten Prinz Rohan
named after Duke Henri of Rohan, Prince of Léon (1579–1638)
who defeated the combined Austrian and Spanish forces 1631–35 in Veltlin

Preparation:

First, carefully clean the goose livers by removing all membranes and silver skin. Then cut the goose livers into strips of approximately the width of a finger and roll in a mixture of sautéed onions, chopped parsley and mushrooms. Skin the roast if necessary and lard with the goose livers by carefully poking holes either with a larding needle or a sharp narrow knife and stuffing them with the goose livers. Season the beef loin with salt and freshly ground pepper. Wrap the meat with the caul that has been first soaked in warm water and then well-dried. Preheat the oven between 400–425 °F (200–220 °C) and bake the loin for 20–40 minutes (to desired temperature) basting frequently and periodically lowering the heat, but do not cook all the way through. Remove the beef, set aside, and keep warm. Strain the drippings and remove the fat if necessary. At this stage you can add water or broth to drippings, let cook thoroughly and bind with butter. Now, cook the roast completely through and subsequently cut into slices and top with sauce.
Recommended Side Dish: shoestring or roast potatoes with green beans and bacon

Ingredients:

3/4 kg (1 1/2 lb.) beef loin
100 g (3 1/2 oz) firm goose livers (replaceable by strips of bacon)
50 g (2 oz) chopped mushrooms
1 Tbs. sautéed onions
chopped parsley
1 pork caul
salt
freshly ground pepper
butter or oil
water or broth
1–2 Tbs. cold butter

Steak for a Princess

Beiried nach Prinzessinnenart

Ingredients:

- 4 top round steaks the thickness of a finger
- oil
- salt
- freshly ground pepper

for the herb butter:

- 100 g (3 1/2 oz) butter
- chopped herbs according to preference (parsley, basil, tarragon, chervil, chives etc.)
- 1 small garlic clove – pressed
- salt
- lemon juice

for the garnish:

- fresh peas (frozen, if not available)
- 100 g (3 1/2 oz) chopped ham
- 500 g (1 lb.) uncooked potatoes
- oil
- butter

Preparation:

Carefully pound out the steaks and let marinate in oil for about 2 hours. In the meantime, make the herb butter with the listed ingredients, form into tube-shaped rolls, wrap in aluminum foil and refrigerate. Before frying the steaks, season them with salt and freshly ground pepper and grill at the desired temperature or fry in a pan. For the garnish, sauté the chopped ham – keep warm. Boil the peas making sure they remain crisp and toss in butter. Cut the potatoes into fine noodle-like strips or wedges and fry in hot oil. Serve the already prepared top round steaks on a platter; fan the sliced butter in a shingle-like fashion over the top and arrange the cubed ham, peas and potatoes around the entrée in a decorative fashion.

Prince Auersperg Rump Steak

Rumpsteak Fürst Auersperg
named after Prince Karl Wilhelm of Auersperg (1814–1890),
1861–1867 president of the Upper Chamber

Ingredients:

- 4 rump steaks cut to the thickness of a finger
- 200 g (7 oz) goose livers (can be replaced with duck or chicken livers)
- 4 slices beef marrow
- 100 g (3 1/2 oz) mushrooms
- salt
- freshly ground pepper
- parmesan cheese
- breadcrumbs
- flour
- butter or oil

Preparation:

Carefully pound out the rump steaks, season with salt and freshly ground pepper and flour on one side. Melt butter in a pan (or heat up oil), and brown the floured side. In the meantime, grease an oven-safe pan with butter, then lay the rump steaks into the pan with the uncooked side down. Clean the goose livers well, cut into slices and arrange over the steaks. Also top the steaks with the slices of beef marrow and sliced mushrooms, sprinkle with breadcrumbs and parmesan cheese, and finally round off with a few slivers of butter. Bake in an oven preheated to 425 °F (220 °C) for approximately 10 minutes until cheese has browned.

Recommended Side Dish: fried potatoes and glazed cauliflower

Steak Esterhàzy

Esterhàzy Rostbraten
named after the Hungarian magnates of the Esterhàzys from Galantha

Preparation:

Thoroughly pound out the steaks and make small incisions on the edges to avert curling of meat while frying. Season with salt and pepper and fry on both sides in hot butter. In the meantime, cut the root vegetables, the onions and sardines into fine, noodle-like strips and dice the bacon. Now in a saucepan, alternately layer in this order: chopped root vegetables, onions, bacon and steaks. The last layer of steak should be topped with root vegetables, a few capers, the sardines, whisked cream and a small amount of beef broth. Place the pan in an oven preheated to approximately 400 °F (200 °C) and braise until tender (about 1 1/2 hours). Remove the steaks from the sauce pan and keep warm. Skim the fat from the steak drippings and if desired, remove the celery strips, which by the way, was quite common during the reign of the Kaisers. Now, whisk together some flour with a small amount of cream or water. To the drippings, add along with the above mixture some salt, a pinch of sugar, lemon juice and more capers if desired. Bring to a boil and continue cooking for several minutes until thick. Top the warm steaks with the sauce and garnish with chopped parsley if desired.
Recommended Side Dish: tarhonya and cucumber salad

Ingredients:

4 steaks (i.e. rib-eyes)
root vegetables (carrots, celery stalk, parsley etc.)
2–3 sardines
chopped capers
1 small onion
50 g (2 oz) bacon
250 ml (8 fluid oz) beef broth
125 ml (4 fluid oz) cream
1 Tbs. flour
cream or water for adjusting consistency
lemon juice
a pinch of sugar
salt
pepper
butter
chopped parsley (optional)

Beef Rolls for the Adjutant

Adjutantenrouladen

Preparation:

Pound out the pork and/or beef cutlets, make small incisions on the sides and season well with salt. Rub the beef cutlets with paprika and brush one side with mustard. Finely chop the bacon and combine with the sardines, capers and the parsley. Spread out the beef cutlets on a countertop with the mustard side facing up and top each with one pork cutlet - coat with the bacon mixture. Roll up the cutlets and fasten them shut with kitchen string. Melt the butter or heat up the oil in a pan, brown the beef rolls on all sides, remove from pan and sauté the onions. Now place the beef rolls back into the pan, add water and cover – braise for 1–1 1/2 hours or until tender. Take the now tender beef rolls out of the pan and keep warm. For the sauce, combine the flour with the cream and then stir into the meat drippings and reduce until all ingredients are well incorporated – this will produce a thick sauce. Cook until the sauce thickens. Season again if desired. Serve the beef rolls, top with the sauce and garnish with parsley.

Recommended Side Dish: Potatoes-Au-Gratin and vegetables

Ingredients:

4 small, thin pork cutlets
4 larger, thin beef cutlets or top round steaks
salt
(sweet) paprika
mustard
80 g (3 oz) semi-lean bacon
2 tsp. chopped sardine filets
1 tsp. chopped capers
2 tsp. chopped parsley
clarified butter or oil
200 g (7 oz) chopped onions
150 ml (5 fluid oz) cream
1–2 Tbs. flour
chopped parsley for garnish

Metternich Tournedos

Tournedos Metternich
named after the Chancellor of the House Metternich, Royal Chancellor of Austria, and Head of State Prince Clemens Wenzel von Metternich

Preparation:

For the risotto, sauté the onions in butter, then add the already rinsed and dried rice. Stir until the rice becomes transparent, season lightly with salt and cover with beef broth. Cook the risotto "al dente" while continuously stirring – always add just enough broth so that the rice is covered. As soon as the rice has become glassy on the outside, but is still white on the inside (this usually takes about 15–20 minutes), the risotto is done. In the meantime, season the steaks with salt and freshly ground pepper and sear in hot oil over an intense flame on both sides to the desired temperature. Remove the steaks (tournedos) from the pan and add water or beef broth to the left over drippings, bring to a boil and complete with cold butter. Cut the already cleaned mushrooms into slices or large pieces and sauté briefly in hot butter. Clean and slice the truffle. Add the truffle slices to the already prepared risotto. The risotto should be served on a platter (or on a serving dish) as the "body". Top with the tournedos and garnish with sautéed mushrooms. Finally, ladle the sauce over the tournedos.

Ingredients:

- 4 beef loin steaks of approx. 150–180 g (5–6 oz)
- 1 truffle, or other mushroom sautéd in butter
- 100 g (3 1/2 oz) mushrooms
- 250 g (9 oz) short-grain rice
- 1 Tbs. chopped onions
- approx. 3/4–1 l (24 - 32 fluid oz) beef broth
- cold slivers of butter for the sauce
- salt
- freshly ground pepper
- butter or oil

KAISER GOULASH

Kaisergulasch

Preparation:

Coarsely cube the steak – here you can certainly make use of the fatty edges for their flavor. Finely chop the onions, heat up the clarified butter or oil and brown the onions while stirring constantly. As soon as the onions have browned, stir in the paprika and dissolve with a dash of vinegar and a small amount of water. For this procedure, it's best to remove the saucepan from the heat, because intense heat may cause the paprika to develop a slightly bitter taste. Return the saucepan to the heat, let cook briefly and then add the meat. Stir in the tomato paste along with all seasoning agents and steam with lid partially open. While this is cooking, the juices should be allowed to reduce several times, whereupon more water should be added. As soon as the meat is tender, stir in the flour and again put in just enough water to cover the meat. Now, cook the sauce in an open pan for several minutes or until the desired consistency and proper fat ratio has been reached.
Recommended Side Dish: according to tradition, Kaiser Goulash has always been served with noodles tossed in butter.

Ingredients:

- 750 g (1 lb. 10 oz) top round steak
- 100 g (3 1/2 oz) clarified butter or oil
- 500 g (1 lb.) onions
- 4 Tbs. sweet paprika
- vinegar
- tomato paste
- 1–2 garlic cloves – pressed
- ground caraway
- marjoram
- salt
- 1 Tbs. flour

Wild Boar - Laxenburger Style

Wildschwein auf Laxenburger Art
named after the moated summer residence of the Habsburgs located in front of the former city walls of Vienna

Preparation:

Remove the chine from the bone, clean well, season with salt, roll up and fasten shut. Coarsely dice the root vegetables and the tomatoes, heat up the oil in a frying pan, and sauté these along with the juniper berries, peppercorns, bay leaves and allspice. Add the rolled boar chine and sear on all sides. Carefully drain the left-over fat and mix in red wine to the drippings, then add just enough broth to completely cover the meat. Braise the roast in an oven preheated between 400–425 °F (200–220 °C) for approximately 90 minutes until tender – lower the heat periodically. Remove the meat and keep warm – now, finish the sauce. To do this, bring to a boil the desired amount of juices along with a small amount of broth, the butter, mustard, jam, chopped mushrooms, and the tarragon. Cook until the sauce thickens and strain through a cheese cloth. Slice the roast, and serve with the sauce.
Recommended Side Dish: a suitable complement, especially popular during the reign of the Kaisers, is freshly picked horseradish, buttered potatoes, and rose-hip sauce.

Ingredients:

makes approx. 6 portions

- 1 chine of young boar of approx. 2 kg (4 lb.)
- salt
- 1 batch of root vegetables (carrots, celery stalk, parsley etc.)
- 3 tomatoes
- juniper berries
- peppercorns
- bay leaves
- whole allspice
- 1/2 l (16 fluid oz) red wine
- broth
- 1 nut-sized piece of butter
- 2 Tbs. cranberry or rose-hip jam
- 1 tsp. Dijon mustard
- 1 Tbs. chopped tarragon
- 2 Tbs. chopped mushrooms
- oil

Pork Loin for a Kaiser

Kaiserkarree

Preparation:

It is best to have the back bone professionally removed by your local butcher. Have an incision made along where the back bone was removed in order to facilitate the stuffing. Open the pork loin (the pork loin should now resemble a crown), salt and rub with garlic. For the stuffing, soak the white bread or rolls in milk or water. In the meantime, melt the butter in a pan and stir in the eggs once the butter has become foamy. Press the liquid from rolls, pass them through a sieve, add to butter along with the breadcrumbs and all spices – mix well. Spread the stuffing into the now open pork loin, roll together and fasten shut. After the outside of the pork loin has been seasoned with salt, garlic and caraway, it should be laid upon the pork bones in a frying pan, preheat the oven to 425 °F (220 °C) and bake for approximately 1 1/2 hours – lower the heat periodically. Be sure to baste the loin regularly with the meat juices and to add water if necessary. Remove the prepared pork loin, skim the excess fat and bring the drippings to a boil. Now, sprinkle flour over the bones, cook briefly, add a small amount of water and let cook shortly once again. Strain the sauce before serving.
Recommended Side Dish: pickled vegetables with peas and a cucumber salad

Ingredients:

- 1 kg (2 lb.) pork loin
- salt
- caraway
- 3–4 crushed garlic cloves
- 500 g (1 lb.) pork bones
- flour
- for the stuffing:
- 4 day old rolls or 8 slices white bread
- milk or water
- 3–4 Tbs. butter
- 3 eggs
- 3 Tbs. breadcrumbs
- salt
- pepper
- nutmeg
- chopped parsley

How to Consume an Entire Province

Although the Congress of Vienna (1814–1815) began as a political event, it ended, as one knows, as a series of wild parties for the attending diplomats, which set the royal kitchen in a state of frenzy. Hans Graf von Schlitz, who attended the congress and possessed an acute sense of perception, documented his impressions during the raging battles along the royal buffet in a remarkably vivid manner: "The endless corpses of fowl, fish, four-legged animals lay lined up along side one another. Many a blazing pit lie in wait for their further preparation. Cooks and kitchen helpers ran about colliding into one another in the chaos, while head chefs loomed over their pots, mixing, separating, shaping and chopping, as though brooding over an artistic scheme for giving the deceased animals, purely natural matter, an alluring taste, smell and appearance. By the way, not just those residing in the Kaiser's castle were being cooked, fried and baked for, but rather also for the entire retinue who also was allowed to invite guests. I was told: It supposedly costs the royal house 500,000 Gulden for every day of congress, which means that the time alone necessary for negotiations to grant one of the provinces peace would probably consume it.

Imperial Opera Style Flitter Mouse

Fledermaus nach Hofopernart

Preparation:

To begin, boil the cleaned "flitter mice" 70–90 minutes in lightly salted water until tender and let cool. In the meantime, melt butter in a saucepan, add flour, brown lightly and pour in milk. Cook the mixture until thick and add the salt, pepper, some lemon juice, horseradish and nutmeg. Remove from heat and bind with egg yolks. Cut the "flitter mice" into approximately 3/4" or 1 cm slices, use these to cover the bottom of a pan and add just enough beef broth to also fill and cover bottom. Spread the sauce over the meat, sprinkle with grated cheese and breadcrumbs, top with a few slivers of butter, and brown approximately 15 minutes in an oven preheated to 425 °F (220 °C).

Recommended Side Dish: potato pasta and fresh spinach

Ingredients:

700 g (1 1/2 lb.) "flitter mouse" pork (especially juicy and semi-lean pork)

beef broth

for the sauce:

2 Tbs. butter

2 Tbs. flour

250 ml (8 fluid oz) milk

lemon juice

ground nutmeg

salt

pepper

grated horseradish

2 egg yolks

for garnish:

grated cheese

breadcrumbs

a few slivers of butter

Maria Theresia's Favorite Dish

Maria Theresias Lieblingsgericht
named after Empress Maria Theresia von Habsburg, Queen of Hungary and Bohemia, regent of the inherited territories (1717–1780)

Preparation:

Bring salted water to a boil, add seasonings, onion and the root vegetables, then boil the chicken for about 1 hour until tender. Remove the chicken from the fond and carefully separate the meat from the bone so that the breast remains whole and can be cut into slices – keep warm after slicing. Dice the remaining meat, then warm up the cow tongue. Now melt the butter in a sauce pan, sauté the rice briefly, add about 4 cups chicken fond, some of the diced chicken (in the meantime, keep the rest warm) and steam until the rice is al dente. Remove the rice from heat and place on a serving dish. Top with the remaining chopped chicken, which will serve as the "basis" for the dish. Now alternately layer with sliced chicken breast, cow tongue and truffle. Finally, thicken the chicken fond with roux and ladle over dish, if desired.
Recommended Side Dish: red leaf or oak leaf lettuce salad

Ingredients:

- 1 cleaned chicken
- salt
- pepper
- 1 batch of root vegetables (carrots, celery stalk, parsley etc.)
- 1 onion
- 1 tsp. peppercorns
- bay leaves
- 2 cups rice
- 1 Tbs. butter
- 200 g (7 oz) cooked cow tongue
- 1 black Périgord-Truffle sliced very thin or cleaned raw mushrooms sliced thin

PHEASANT À LA LERCHENAU

Fasan Ochs auf Lerchenau
named after the Baron from the opera "The Rose Cavalier"
by Richard Strauss (1864–1949)

Preparation:

It is best to have the pheasants wrapped with bacon by your local butcher. Sear the pheasant on all sides. Lay the pheasant on top of the seasonings and chopped shallots in a saucepan – pour in the broth and the wine. Preheat the oven to 140°C (285°F) and slowly roast the pheasant for 1 1/2 to 2 hours. Remove the cooked pheasant from the pan, add a small amount of flour to the drippings, heat through and add a bit of broth or wild game fond if desired. Reduce the sauce to the desired consistency and strain – ladle over carved pheasant.
Recommended Side Dish: mashed potatoes and red cabbage

Ingredients:

1–2 (depending on size)
pheasants wrapped with bacon
4 shallots (or small onions)
allspice
cloves
bay leaves
peppercorns
broth or wild game fond
150 ml (5 fluid oz) Tokay wine
(or any full-bodied white wine)
flour

• Häferlgucker •

The King Who Roasted Chickens

The fact that Kaisers and Kings made sure to always feast upon the finest delicacies does not necessarily need special mention in a book dealing with imperial cuisine. It is far more seldom to find crowned heads who prepare their own roast. This was done – quite against his will – by the king of Briton Richard the Lionheart (1157–1199). Namely during the time when he went to work as a chicken cook in a hunting lodge, which stood in front of the former walls of the city of Vienna. He was fleeing from his adversary Margrave Leopold V (1157–1194) and was forced to do this in order to maintain his secret identity. He forgot, however, to remove his sovereign ring and was, as is stated in the chronicles, arrested at the lowly position of chicken cook. While he was being arrested, and even before he was taken to the fortress prison in Dürnstein, he offered the evidence more or less *in flagranti* – chickens from the Viennese forest were also quite popular about 900 years ago.

Mini-Meat Loaves for Imperial Hunters

Kaiserjägerlaibchen

Ingredients:

- 700 g (1 1/2 lb.) ground meat (lean beef and pork)
- 1 1/2 day old rolls or 3 slices white bread
- 1 large onion
- 2 eggs
- 2 crushed garlic cloves
- marjoram
- salt
- pepper
- chopped parsley
- 1–2 Tbs. breadcrumbs
- clarified butter or oil
- breadcrumbs

for the sauce:

- 250 g (9 oz) mushrooms
- 1 Tbs. finely chopped onions
- 2 Tbs. butter
- 150 ml (5 fluid oz) whipping cream
- 150 ml (5 fluid oz) beef broth
- 150 (5 fluid oz) cream
- 1 tsp. flour
- salt
- freshly ground pepper
- chopped parsley
- lemon juice

Preparation:

Finely chop the onion, sauté in hot oil, and let cool. In the meantime, soak the rolls or white bread in cold water, press out thoroughly and pass through a sieve. Now combine the ground meat, the rolls, the eggs, the sauteed onions, breadcrumbs, and all seasonings. Wet hands and form small loaves. Coat loaves with breadcrumbs, heat up the clarified butter or oil in a large pan, and fry on both sides until golden brown. In the meantime, slice the mushrooms and finely chop the onions for the sauce. Remove the meat loaves from the pan, keep warm, and drain the fat. Melt butter in the same pan until foamy and lightly sauté the onions, then add the mushrooms, cook briefly and finally season with salt and pepper. Add whipping cream, beef broth and bring to a boil. Mix the flour and the cream separately and stir into the sauce. Bring again to a boil, and finish with chopped parsley, lemon juice and, if need be, salt and pepper once the sauce is thick. Top the loaves with the mushroom sauce and serve.

Recommended Side Dish: potato croquettes and glazed baby carrots

Christofle
FRANCE

Sweets From the "Komposterey"

The legendary reputation of Viennese baked goods can be largely attributed to the Habsburg-Kaiser Ferdinand I, who grew up in Spain and took up residence on the Danube in 1522. Although Ferdinand was enthusiastic about Viennese cuisine, he missed the variety of sweet treats he was used to receiving ever since his childhood from the Dutch confectioner who was employed at the Spanish court. And so he had a so-called "Komposterey" opened in order to have jams and fruit juices made, for which he summoned to the Viennese court proven "Zuggermacher" or confectioners from the Netherlands and Spain. The Dutchman Matthias de Viss stepped in as the first Viennese court confectioner in 1560. The first Viennese confectioners' guild had already been established five years previous to this in 1555 and had also found a benevolent patron in Kaiser Ferdinand. By the way, the extent to which the ruling House of Austria had affection for anything sweet can be affirmed even today by the fact that there is actually a "confectioners' stairway" at the royal castle in Vienna.

Heavenly Desserts from the Imperial Kitchen

Desserts aus dem K.U.K. Mehlspeishimmel

Kaiser Pancakes

Kaiserschmarren

Preparation:

Separate the egg whites from the yolks. Thoroughly mix the yolks, sugar, milk and flour. Whisk the egg whites, add a pinch of salt and continue whisking until stiff. Now, carefully fold into the egg yolk mixture. Melt butter in a large pan, pour in the mixture and sprinkle in raisins. Let cook on one side for a few minutes, turn over and tear into pieces with a fork. Now let finish cooking (ideally in a buttered pan in a preheated oven). Be especially careful not to overcook the pancakes, otherwise they will dry out. Sprinkle with confectioners' sugar and serve with plum purée.

Ingredients:

- 6 eggs
- 200 g (7 oz) cake or pastry flour
- 50 g (1 1/2 oz) sugar
- 250 ml (8 fluid oz) milk
- pinch of salt
- 40 g (1 oz) raisins
- butter
- confectioners' sugar (powdered)
- plum purée

Omelette Schönbrunn

Omelette Schönbrunn
named after the Kaiser's summer residence in Vienna-Hietzing

Preparation:

Thoroughly whisk together the milk and whipping cream, add a pinch of salt, and heat together with the butter in a sauce pan. After mixture has begun to boil, add the flour and at an even temperature stir constantly until the mixture no longer adheres to the sides of the pan. While the mixture is cooling, separate the egg yolks from the whites, add the crystal sugar to the whites and whisk until stiff. Stir in the egg yolks and approximately 1/2 of the whisked egg whites to the milk/cream mixture. Now, carefully work in the rest of the egg whites. Melt butter in a pan, add enough of the batter each time for one small omelette and lightly brown, turn over and carefully finish cooking the omelettes over low heat. Don't overcook, otherwise the omelettes will dry out. Spread the jam over half of each prepared omelette, fold together diagonally, sprinkle with confectioners' sugar and serve.

Ingredients:

makes 5–6 portions

200 ml (6 1/2 fluid oz) milk

100 ml (3 fluid oz) whipping cream

2 Tbs. butter

2–3 Tbs. flour

5 eggs

3 Tbs. coarse or crystal sugar

salt

butter

apricot jam

confectioners' sugar

"Leopold, Hand Over the Pancakes"

Numerous rumors and anecdotes circulate about the origin of Kaiser pancakes, and the only thread they have in common is that they haven't been confirmed. One anecdote tells of a court confectioner by the name of Leopold who one day merrily presented the royal family with a composition consisting of omelette batter and plum purée. The empress, who was watchful of her waistline, took a taste, wrinkled her nose and refused to take another bite. The Kaiser, however, felt sorry for his confectioner and ate up the empress's portion with the words, "Just give me the pancakes that our confectioner cooked up." A different story takes place during the imperial hunt and tells about an alpine dairyman, also called a "Kaser", in whose hut the hunters take a rest. The only thing available in the hut to eat was plain "Kaser" pancakes, which tasted so good to the Kaiser that this dish in no time at all was raised to the noble rank of Kaiser Pancakes. In the end, many culinary historians also want to know how the often quoted Kaiser's favorite dish came to be named after the Casa de Austria or the Royal House of Austria. Supposedly these Kaiser Pancakes originated at some point in time from these "Pancakes à la Casa".

Count Meran Plum Dumplings

Zwetschkenknödel Graf von Meran
named after Count Fanz von Meran and Baron von Brandhof,
son of Archduke Johann (1839–1891)

Preparation:

Boil the potatoes until soft, peel, and pass them through a sieve while still warm. On a counter combine flour, semolina, 3 oz butter, eggs, potatoes and a pinch of salt – knead into a smooth dough. Clean the plums, remove the pits and place a piece of marzipan (or a sugar cube with some cinnamon) into the center. Roll out the dough to a thickness of approximately 5 cm (2"), cut into slices and press flat. Wrap up one plum in each of the slices and make sure to carefully and completely seal all edges. Bring lightly salted water to a boil and simmer the dumplings for 8 to 12 minutes. In the meantime, melt butter in a pan until foamy, add the breadcrumbs and sauté until golden brown. Strain the prepared dumplings and carefully roll in the butter/breadcrumb mixture. Sprinkle with confectioners' sugar and serve.

Ingredients:

makes approx. 25 dumplings

1 kg (2 lb.) potatoes

300 g (10 1/2 oz) flour

80 g (3 oz) butter

2 eggs

1 Tbs. semolina

salt

approx. 25 plums

150 g (5 oz) butter

130 g (4 1/2 oz) breadcrumbs

plain marzipan (or this can be replaced with 1 sugar cube & some cinnamon for each dumpling)

confectioners' sugar

Rice à la Prince Trautmansdorff

Reis nach Fürst Trautmansdorff
named after Count Ferdinand von Traumansdorff,
Head Chamberlain and first president of the Upper Chamber (1825–1896)

Preparation:

First, rinse rice and cook in 1 l of water (32 fluid oz) for 6–7 minutes, drain, add cold milk and bring to a boil. Stir in a pinch of salt and the vanilla sugar – steam until tender (ideally in an oven at approx. 285 °F (140 °C)). In the meantime, finely chop the fruit and marinate in the alcohol. Soften the gelatin leaves in water, press out and stir into the hot rice along with the sugar. While the rice is cooling, whip the cream until it peaks. Shortly before the rice begins to clump, combine with the marinated fruit. Place the rice into small soufflé dishes which have been rinsed with cold water and let cool for several hours. Before serving, turn over the soufflé dishes to dislodge the rice – garnish with whipped cream, candied fruit or fruit purée as desired.

Ingredients:

- 70 g (2 1/2 oz) short-grain rice
- 250 ml (8 fluid oz) heavy cream
- 250 ml (8 fluid oz) milk
- 2 Tbs. sugar
- 4 gelatin leaves
- 200–300 g (7–10 oz) fruit (pears, berries, grapes etc.)
- vanilla sugar
- pinch of salt
- Maraschino liqueur or cognac
- whipped cream
- candied fruit or fruit purée

Imperial Fritters for the Fasching Ball

Hofball-Faschingskrapfen

Preparation:

In a small bowl dissolve yeast in approximately 2 Tbs. warm milk, add a small amount of flour and a pinch of sugar, and finally place the smaller bowl into a larger bowl partially filled with warm water. Set aside in a warm area and let rise until the dough has doubled in size. In the meantime, combine the egg yolks with the remaining sugar and stir until foamy. Now, heat up the rest of the milk until lukewarm, and stir this into the egg yolk mixture along with the melted butter, salt, vanilla sugar, rum, and grated lemon peel. Add the dough and the remaining flour and stir briskly until the dough starts to form bubbles and no longer adheres to the sides. Sprinkle a small amount of flour over the dough and set aside in a warm area for approximately 1/2 hour (During this entire process, as well as during the actual frying of the fritters, one should pay close attention that no draft of any kind exists and that the room maintains a constant temperature). After the dough has been allowed to rise, once again firmly knead the dough and form fritters of about 6–7 cm (2–3 inches) in diameter, which should be placed on a kitchen towel sprinkled with flour and allowed to rise for a good 1/2 hour. Heat up the oil, place the fritters in the oil and briefly fry in a covered vessel. After about 3 minutes turn the fritters over and finish frying them uncovered. Remove the fritters and let drain and cool on a rack. In the meantime, strain the apricot jam and stir in a shot of rum or apricot schnapps if desired – fill the pastry bag with the jam and inject into the slightly cooled fritters. Lastly, sprinkle with confectioners' sugar.

Ingredients:

makes approx. 20 Fritters
- 280 g (10 oz) flour (either all-purpose, or 1/2 pastry flour and 1/2 all purpose)
- 50 g (2 oz) butter
- 100 ml (3 fluid oz) milk
- 4 egg yolks
- 20 g (1/2 oz) yeast
- 30 g (1 oz) sugar
- pinch of salt
- vanilla sugar
- lemon peel
- shot of rum
- flour for sprinkling
- clarified butter or oil
- apricot jam
- confectioners' sugar

The Kaiser's Guardsmen

Kaisergardisten

Preparation:

Combine flour, vanilla sugar, the egg, egg yolk, and quickly knead into a dough. Roll out the dough to the thickness of a knife handle and divide into strips of approximately 8 cm (3") in width. With the halved almonds form two rows in the center of the dough strips, fold the long sides over each other and seal. Lay the dough strips tops down onto a greased sheet tray. Brush with egg white and bake in an oven preheated to 400 °F (200 °C) for approximately 10 minutes. Slice the "Kaiser's Guardsmen" into very thin strips while still warm.

Ingredients:

140 g (5 oz) flour
140 g (5 oz) vanilla sugar
1 egg
1 egg yolk
80–100 g (3–3 1/2 oz) shelled and halved almonds
butter
1 egg white

Frau Cilly's Temptations

The main attraction at the Viennese royal balls, besides the famous Olio stew, exists thanks not to an aristocrat, but rather to a commoner, namely the cook Cäcilie Krapf. The word "Krapfen" or "doughnut" (contrary to common legend) does not originate from her, but rather from the recipe for "Craphen", which stems from as far back as the middle ages and were variations of "Cillykugeln" – jam-filled balls – the actual predecessors of today's Fasching doughnuts. The "Krapfen" or doughnut proved to be a sweet best-seller in every sense of the word long before the advent of the Sachertorte: According to statistics from the royal kitchen, around 10,000,000 "Krapfen" were consumed at official receptions and balls in the congressional year of 1815 alone.

Empress Elisabeth's Afternoon Snack

Kaiserin Elisabeths Nachmittagsnäscherei

Preparation:

Combine the flour and butter – texture should be crumbly. Add almonds, crystal sugar, and the egg and quickly knead into a dough. Roll out the dough to the thickness of a knife handle and divide into two long sheets with a width of approximately 8 cm (3"). Place the dough sheets on an ungreased sheet pan and bake in an oven preheated to 400 °F (200 °C) for approximately 10 minutes. In the meantime, dissolve the sugar in the water and then bring to a boil without stirring. Now, skim the unsightly foam which rises to the top. Continue cooking the sugar. Take a silver spoon, dip first in cold water, then in the sugar mixture and once more in the cold water – repeat this procedure until the sugar forms a smooth, firm ball on the spoon. Whip the egg whites until stiff, stir into the hot (purified) sugar, and put the pot into ice water. Stir until the mixture has chilled. Fold the strawberry purée into the sugar solution and spread over the dough sheets. Bake in a hot oven for a few seconds until the frosting has begun to slightly dry and stick to the dough sheets. Remove from the oven and drizzle with chocolate glaze. Finally, cut the dough sheets into individual portions.

Ingredients:

200 g (7 oz) flour
140 g (5 oz) butter
70 g (2 1/2 oz) coarse or crystal sugar
70 g (2 1/2 oz) ground almonds
1 egg
chocolate glaze
for the frosting:
280 g (10 oz) sugar
125 ml (4 fluid oz) water
8 egg whites
150 g (5 oz) strawberry purée

A Violet Sorbet for Empress Elisabeth

The Empress Elisabeth, who tended more to anorexia than to gorging herself, was as heaven knows no source of thanks for ambitious royal cooks. She spent her whole life wanting to shed weight, most preferred to nourish herself from sour milk and was often seen drinking ox blood, which she regarded as especially invigorating. It was only during breakfast that the empress failed to resist temptation. She would consume, if one lends credence to the reports of the royal kitchen, one plate of fruit, three rolls, a quarter pound of sugar, a quarter pound of butter, a pitcher each of cream, cold milk, and coffee, and a piece of gugelhupf cake or a "Pischinger roll" along with a full plate of sweet pastries, cookies and chocolate. From then on she would starve herself with iron discipline, that is unless she once again craved something sweet. In which case she would have a sorbet from the neighboring bakery Demel brought to her chambers, which consisted of the juices of a pressed violet, spun sugar and a few dashes of champagne.

Bad Ischl Tartlets

Bad Ischler Törtchen

Preparation:

Work the butter into the flour – texture will be crumbly. Add sugar, almonds, salt, and cinnamon and quickly knead into a dough – set aside in a cool place. Roll out the dough to approximately 3 mm (1/10") thick and cut out circles with a radius of 5–6 cm (2–2 1/2"). Preheat the oven to 400 °F (200 °C) and bake the cookies approximately 10 minutes. In the meantime, make the cream by melting butter in a pot until foamy, mixing in confectioners' sugar, chocolate that has been melted in a double boiler, and a shot of rum. Distribute current jam and chocolate cream over half of the cooled tartlets (ideally this is done with a pastry bag) and top with the second half of the tartlets sandwich style. Drizzle the warm chocolate glaze over the tartlets and sprinkle with chopped pistachios or almonds.

Ingredients:

- 140 g (5 oz) butter
- 140 g (5 oz) flour
- 70 g (2 1/2 oz) sugar
- 70 g (2 1/2 oz) ground almonds
- cinnamon
- pinch of salt
- current jam
- chocolate glaze
- chopped pistachios or almonds

for the filling:

- 150 g (5 oz) butter
- 2 Tbs. confectioners' sugar
- 60 g (2 oz) chocolate
- shot of rum

Margarethe's Sweet Pastry Squares

Margarethes Süße Maultaschen
named after Margarethe Maultasch, Countess of Tyrol (1318–1369)

Preparation:

Combine egg yolk, flour, butter, sugar and wine, knead into a smooth dough and let rest for one half hour. Roll out the dough to the thickness of knife handle and cut into squares. Place a heaping teaspoon of the fruit compote or spread jam in the center of each of the squares. Now, fold the four corners of the dough towards the center being sure that the fruit or jam is still visible. Beat the egg and brush onto the squares. Sprinkle the coarse sugar and almonds over the squares – bake in an oven preheated to 400 °F (200 °C) until golden brown (approx. 10 minutes).

Ingredients:

- 1 egg yolk
- 140 g (5 oz) flour
- 140 g (5 oz) butter
- 2 Tbs. sugar
- 2 Tbs. white wine
- jam or coarsely chopped fruit compote (apricots, plums, etc.)
- 1 egg
- coarse sugar
- chopped or sliced almonds

Kaiser Ferdinand's Northline Doughnuts

Kaiser Ferdinands Nordbahnkrapferl
named after the Kaiser Ferdinand Northline Railroad, opened in 1837

Preparation:

Separate the egg whites from the yolks and melt the chocolate in a double-boiler. Melt butter in a pan until foamy and stir in the egg yolks, melted chocolate, sugar and aromatics. Whip the egg whites until stiff and fold into the egg yolk mixture – stir in the almonds. Grease a sheet tray with butter, sprinkle with flour (or line with wax paper), spread the mixture on the tray to the thickness of a thumb and preheat the oven to 400 °F (200 °C) and bake the mixture approximately 10 minutes – let cool. With the aid of a cookie cutter, cut out doughnuts with a radius of approximately 4–5 cm (1 1/2 to 2"). Whisk the whipping cream until peaks form, spread onto half of the doughnuts and top the rest with jam. Place the doughnuts with jam onto the doughnuts with whipped cream (sandwich-style, so that the filling is in the middle). Top with lemon or sugar glaze and decorate with a candied cherry.

Ingredients:

6 eggs
150 g (5 oz) butter at room temperature
100 g (3 1/2 oz) chocolate
200 g (7 oz) sugar
200 g (7 oz) ground almonds
lemon peel
cinnamon
ground cloves
butter and flour for the pan
for the filling:
250 ml (8 fluid oz) whipping cream
jam
lemon or sugar glaze
candied cherries

Steinkogler Gugelhupf

Steinkogler Gugelhupf

Preparation:

Combine yeast, a small amount of warm milk, a pinch of sugar, and 1 Tbs. flour in a mixing bowl and keep warm. Then melt butter in pan and stir until foamy. Now, mix in the sugar, egg yolks, flour, milk, pinch of salt and the yeast mixture – stir vigorously until the batter forms bubbles and no longer adheres to the sides. Beat the egg whites until stiff and fold in. Grease a Gugelhupf mold with butter, dust with flour and sprinkle in the almond slivers. Pour in the batter, cover and let rest in a warm location. Meanwhile, preheat the oven to 340–350 °F (170–180 °C) and bake the Gugelhupf for about 1 hour, sprinkle with confectioners' sugar and serve.

Ingredients:

150 g (5 oz) butter
100 g (3 1/2 oz) sugar
6 egg yolks
350 g (1 lb.) flour
approx. 250 ml (8 fluid oz) milk
30 g (1 oz) yeast
2 egg whites
pinch of salt
butter to grease pan
flour for dusting
almond slivers
confectioners' sugar

• *Häferlgucker* •

Royal Culinary Erotica

Although Kaiser Franz Joseph was no gourmet, he was all the more a sweet-tooth, which is corroborated by numerous anecdotes. Katarina Schratt, the famous royal actress and soul-mate of the Kaiser, knew this and had a Gugelhupf cake delivered from the bakery Zauner to his summer residence in Bad Ischl whenever he came to visit. As soon as the Kaiser left this Tête a Tête or heart to heart he would hike over the Steinkogl mountain towards lake Ofen to go hunting, after which the whispering began: "The Kaiser has just ravished another Steinkogler Gugelhupf!", gossiped the locals – and with this statement they expressed in a very decent manner their skepticism whether the Gugelhupf cake was the only thing that His Majesty had just ravished.

A Torte for His Excellency

Exzellenztorte

Preparation:

Melt butter in a pan, stir until foamy, add sugar, eggs, egg yolks, and ground almonds. Whisk the egg whites until stiff and carefully add these alternately along with the breadcrumbs to the egg yolk mixture. In the meantime, melt the chocolate in a double-boiler. Divide the batter in half, pour the first half in a well greased and floured torte mold. Now mix the second half into the melted chocolate and place in a separate torte mold that has been greased and dusted with flour. Preheat the oven to 350 °F (180 °C) and bake the torte bases 40–50 minutes – let slightly cool. Now spread jam over the top of the torte which hasn't been mixed with chocolate. Place the chocolate torte on top of the other and drizzle with a transparent glaze.

Ingredients:

- 250 g (9 oz) butter at room temperature
- 180 g (6 oz) sugar
- 2 eggs
- 8 egg yolks
- 180 g (6 oz) ground almonds
- 8 egg whites
- 100 g (3 1/2 oz) breadcrumbs
- 120 g (4 oz) chocolate
- butter and flour to coat torte pan
- raspberry or current jam
- sugar or lemon glaze

The Chocolate Léver (Breakfast Reception)

That chocolate enjoyed great popularity at the court of Maria Theresia is proven not only by the fact that the court poet and opera librettist Pietro Metastasio (1698–1782) composed a chocolate cantata with his song "Cantata à la Cioccolata", but also in that Empress Maria Theresia's golden vessels for serving chocolate including small serving pitchers, cups, cocoa mugs, spoons and sugar dispensers can still be found today in the Museum of Art and History in Vienna. By the way, one can also find the remarkably revealing watercolor painting of a Chocolate Léver, which was painted by none other than Archduchess Maria Christine herself. The example that the Empress and the Kaiser are setting with their children and a lady of the court as they receive the breakfast chocolate proves to be deceiving when one is more familiar with the lifestyle of the Maria Theresia household. In the day to day routine it wasn't as sweet as sugar like in the painting: Maria Theresia usually drank coffee, the pack of imperial children was tamed with barley-gruel – Prince Consort Franz Stephan von Lothringen was the only one who never began a day without a cup of cocoa.

Count Apponyi-Torte

Graf Apponyi-Torte
named after the Hungarian line of nobility
which produced several significant Austro-Hungarian politicians

Preparation:

Beat the egg whites until stiff and stir in the confectioners' sugar. Carefully fold in the hazelnuts, ground chocolate, and the flour. Preheat the oven to 400 °F (200 °C). Either divide the mixture into fourths and bake four separate crusts (approx. 10 minutes), or bake one large crust (approx. 40 minutes) and divide after having let cooled. The chocolate cream can be prepared in the meantime by combining the eggs, sugar and water in a double-boiler and stirring until foamy. Now, place bowl in an ice-bath and continue stirring until completely cool. Melt the chocolate in a double-boiler, melt butter in a pan and stir until foamy – combine both with the egg mixture. Now, cut each cooled crust into perfect hexagons, spread the cream over each crust and stack. Cover the top layer with cream and garnish with chopped pistachios. Spread chocolate cream on the sides and decorate with vertical rows of hollow wafers.

Ingredients:

- 10 egg whites
- 160 g (5 1/2 oz) confectioners' sugar
- 50 g (2 oz) ground hazelnuts
- 120 g (4 oz) ground chocolate
- 30 g (1 oz) flour

for the chocolate cream:

- 5 egg yolks
- 200 g (7 oz) sugar
- 1 1/2 Tbs. water
- 150 g (5 oz) chocolate
- 200 g (7 oz) butter
- chopped pistachios and hollow wafers

Stephanie's Cream Torte

Stephanie-Cremetorte
named after the daughter of King Leopold II of Belgium (1864–1945),
widow of Crown Prince Rudolf and future Countess of Lonyay

Ingredients:

4 eggs, 170 g (6 oz) sugar
100 g (3 1/2 oz) ground hazelnuts
100 g (3 1/2 oz) ground chocolate
butter
flour
125 ml (4 oz) whipped cream
2 Tbs. sugar
chopped pistachios
for the chocolate cream:
60 g (2 oz) chocolate
60 g (2 oz) sugar
approx. 80 ml (2 1/2 fluid oz) water
125 ml (4 oz) whipping cream
2 gelatin leaves
for the hazelnut cream:
125 ml (4 fluid oz) whipping cream
3 egg yolks
70 g (2 1/2 oz) sugar
70 g (2 1/2 oz) ground hazelnuts
125 ml (4 oz) whipped cream
2 gelatin leaves
for the raspberry cream:
125 ml (4 fluid oz) whipping cream
70 g (2 1/2 oz) raspberry purée
2 gelatin leaves

Preparation:

For the torte base separate the egg whites from the egg yolks, combine the yolks with the sugar and stir until foamy. Beat the egg whites until stiff and stir into the egg yolk mixture along with the ground hazelnuts and ground chocolate. Now preheat the oven to 350 °F (180 °C) and bake a total of four torte bases in a greased and floured springform pan – either 1 at a time using a quarter of the batter or by spreading out four circles on wax paper and trimming after baking (bake each for approx. 10 minutes). Remove the tortes from the springform pan or from the wax paper while still warm and fill with the cream which is to be prepared in the meantime. For the chocolate cream, combine sugar and water and boil until sugar is "spun" (see also p. 102) or has reached the soft crack stage. In order to confirm that the correct consistency has been reached, dip a spoon into in the water and touch it with the index finger. Now, touch your thumb with your index finger and slowly separate. If a long thread forms between thumb and index finger which resists breaking, the correct consistency has been reached. Dissolve the gelatin in water, mix into the sugar along with chocolate that has been melted in a double-boiler, and whipped cream – stir until smooth.

For the hazelnut cream, whisk the whipping cream, egg yolks, sugar and ground hazelnuts in a double-boiler until the cream has thickened. Afterwards, soften the gelatin leaves in

water, press out the excess water and stir into the cooled egg yolk mixture. Beat the egg whites until stiff and fold them in as well.
For the raspberry cream, soften the gelatin leaves in water and then dissolve with a few drops of warm water. Combine with the already whipped cream and raspberry purée.
Spread hazelnut cream onto the top of the first torte base, raspberry cream onto the second, and chocolate cream onto the third. Now, layer the tortes one on top of the other. The top of the torte as well as the sides should be spread with cream that has been sweetened and whipped. Lastly, garnish the top and sides with chopped pistachios.

HUNYADY-BOMBE

Hunyady-Bombe
named after the Hungarian line of kings whose ancestry traces back to Johannes Corvinus Hunyady (1385–1456)

Preparation:

Finely sift the confectioners' sugar into the vanilla sugar, combine with the egg yolks and stir until foamy. Either finely grate the chocolate or melt in a double-boiler, then alternately mix chocolate in the egg yolk mixture along with chestnut cream. Beat the egg whites until stiff, fold in as well. Grease two springform pans or torte molds and fill each with an even amount of the mixture. Preheat the oven to 350 °F (180 °C). Bake each torte base individually or both at the same time in a convection oven for approx. 15–20 minutes – let cool. Cut both torte bases horizontally or leave whole if desired. Spread one torte base with apricot jam or chestnut cream according to personal taste and top with the other base (if you have four bases repeat this procedure). Quickly cover the bombe with chocolate ice-cream, decorate with chopped pine nuts and serve immediately. Of course, the chocolate ice-cream can be replaced by a butter-chocolate cream.

Ingredients:

- 8 egg yolks
- 8 egg whites
- 280 g (10 oz) confectioners' sugar
- 140 g (5 oz) chocolate
- 560 g (1 lb. 4 oz) fresh chestnuts (cooked and passed through a sieve) or frozen riced chestnuts
- 1 package vanilla sugar
- butter
- apricot jam or chestnut cream (a mixture of whipped cream and riced chestnuts)
- chocolate ice-cream
- chopped pine nuts

The End of the Court Confectioner

Despite Kaiser Franz Joseph's much publicized love of Gugelhupf cake and Kaiser pancakes, the monarch's Spartan blood seems after all to have been stronger than his passion for sweets. The proud dozen imperial confectioners who were still employed in the royal bakery in 1880 were reduced to a pathetic quartet in 1912. The death-knell struck for the once prestigious royal bakery with the gradually approaching end of the Austro-Hungarian Empire: the pastry chef at the time, Franz Pfitzner, was "demoted" to royal cook first class – by the end of the war the royal bakery was simply shut down once and for all.

rechberger

The following have appeared in the series *Kulinarium (The Culinary)*:

• Imperial Austrian Cuisine
• Aus Kaisers Küche (see above)
• Aus Pfarrers Küche (Pastor's Cuisine)
• Hausmannskost (Simple Cuisine)

Fine kitchenware for these original Austrian cookbooks was provided by:

Firma Rechberger GesmbH
Specialty manufacturer of glass, porcelain, household and kitchen supplies
A-4040 Linz/Urfahr, Ferihumerstraße 6
Tel. 0732/731413, 732175
Fax 0732/732175-22

Many thanks to Firma Rechberger.

• *Notes* •

• Notes •

• *Notes* •

Renate Wagner-Wittula,
born in Addis Abeba, studied German literature and cultural management, has worked for years in a firm which publishes restaurant guides and cookbooks, mother of two children and passionate cook, author of several travel guides and various cookbooks, lives in Vienna

Christoph Wagner,
born in Linz, gourmet journalist and author of numerous cookbooks and works dealing with gastronomy; regular gourmet columnist for the magazine *Profil*; publisher of *Christoph Wagner's Restaurant und Wirtshaus Guide (Christoph Wagner's Restaurant and Inn Guide)*, lives in Vienna